AF322642

PARENTING WITH PURPOSE

PARENTING WITH PURPOSE

Nurturing Happy, Confident Kids

AVERY NIGHTINGALE

Creative Quill Press

CONTENTS

Copyright © 2024 by Avery Nightingale

All rights reserved. No part of this book may be reproduced in any manner whatsoever without written permission except in the case of brief quotations embodied in critical articles and reviews.

First Printing, 2024

CHAPTER 1

Introduction

The author has collected effective and powerful real-world parenting ideas, strategies, and her advice is clear. The narrative flows as the book is easy to navigate, as it addresses what is most important in child development. Michele draws on her experience, wisdom, and knowledge to explain what works and why it works. Parents and educators will gain headings for kids by reading her book. Parenthood is not an exact science, but we can definitely do it with grace and determination under the right guidance, which Michele shares with us in her personal narrative and stories. In Parenting with Purpose, you'll gain self-awareness, how to accept that your child is unique, and how to appreciate those differences. And if we do so, we can become supporters of nurturing well-adjusted, confident, and kind children who confidently seek to find their path in all of our turbulent lives. That is the power of purposeful parenting.

Parenting with Purpose is a must-read book for today's parents. Grounded in a deep understanding of child development, the author's stories bring age-old advice to life in the contemporary world. She shares her remarkable insight supported by cutting-edge findings in neuroscience. This book inspires, challenges, and forges a clear path to creative parenting. Savvy recognized the power of technology and its addictive effect on the young minds. The youth who have misdirected energy are harming not only themselves, but their families are affected as well. Mastering these challenges requires ignoring the quick fixes, setting aside popular ideologies, and utilizing the most effective parenting strategies that seem to be timeless.

CHAPTER 2

Building a Strong Parent-Child Relationship

Supportive parenting is one of the seven expected protective factors for the ACE study that are essential to childhood development and ultimately lead to healthy adulthood. The other six guiding factors were physical autonomy, use of coping skills, encouragement to make decisions, strong support network, use of leadership skills, and social/emotional competence. The first and most important responsibility of any parent is to provide food, warmth, water, and shelter. As adoption is often difficult and completely exhausting, it is frequently overlooked. A good relationship with your adopted child will create a solid non-caring environment for the development of your child through all the achievements and failures.

The way certain behaviors are interpreted involves feelings. However, the feelings parents and children experience in response to their behaviors are not always connected. Parents who criticize their children's behaviors can encourage continued engagement, improve behavioral control, stimulate children's ability to think, or encourage the development of internal control - the most important attribute children have in leading healthy development. Being familiar with your child will help determine how your discipline style affects them. For the most part, the principles are based on children's age, parents' discipline-related ideological beliefs, and the ability to raise a voice without anger or criticism will have positive results.

2.1. Effective Communication

Communication is complex, and it consists of many skills, all of which need to be carefully cultivated. Boys and girls have so much to say, they do it with a great deal of enthusiasm and non-stop too. There is nothing better than a good chat at the table after dinner, while doing small chores together with an adult, or if it rains, constructing an amusing board game. We must listen to them, really listen to the words. During difficult moments, such as when they are not in the mood, and during painful moments where we have to talk about loss, the authority of mothers, just like the elusive quality of love, is shown through the choice of words and the ability to listen and be silent when required. In reality, listening is a form of respect. Indeed, closely connected relationships with our children can only arise from mutual, deep, intimate, and respectful relationships.

One of the habits that plays an essential role in the parent-child relationship is undoubtedly effective communication. Effective communication catalyzes every other important habit: listening, cooperation, shows of empathy, and youthful desire to loosen up and take silly things lightly. The way we communicate makes or breaks a good relationship. Good communication obviously isn't a matter of taking turns to say in an appointment kind of style everything there is to say and then disconnect until your turn comes again. Real communication requires listening to each other, understanding emotions, and how important it is to vent negative emotions, look for solutions to problems, and chat lightly. When you look closely, the exact definition of effective communication is talking, showing empathy, listening, seeking solutions, laughing. Scattered amidst all these lovely gestures are strong signs of love.

2.2. Spending Quality Time Together

In our house, we have a strict "No Screen" day. During this day, we engage in games that encourage talking and good thought-provoking conversation. We play Scrabble and Monopoly, have long baths and good chats - and time for a little on the couch reading. (Sometimes in quiet contemplation, I might even have the luxury of dozing off for a few minutes). The ultimate fun is, of course, in helping create a new recipe and cooking dinner together. Cooking a meal till in the oven is always a joint slow walk outside to spot the flowers that Emily has grown. Getting outside is a great way to connect. It's also a good way to learn to 'just be' and to enjoy the present moment. What do we tend to do when we aren't filling our time with technology and social media (talking more about us than about our children)? Our "no screen" day is about very 'simple' and 'present' activities that bring pleasure and enjoyment. My fondest hope is that one or many elements of this day might, in the future, inspire Emily to feelings of security and comfort when she is stressed.

Busy-ness doesn't always equate to productivity. Busy-ness can be about being stressed, running around from one event to another, and never quite being in the moment. Productivity means actually getting things done and having headspace for the more important things. And what are the more important things? Family time certainly, but also having time for relaxing and even for problem solving and coming up with new creative ideas! It's important not to be too hard on ourselves to get 'everything' done. When your child doesn't reach a weekly soccer goal, don't get angry and push. Get supportive! The bottom line? Manage your time so you can be there, at the right moment, for your child. Pushing and prodding might get short-term results, but in the long run, avoidance increases. Make time for the things that are important. And dear parents, your children are very important.

CHAPTER 3

Promoting Emotional Well-being

Children whose parents inspire in them confidence and the ability to express their emotions will grow to become successful adults. They trust in their ability to cope with trial; they are resilient, which leads them to improbabilities of indulging in risky situations, at times with dire consequences. Other kids, such as those raised by parents who are overbearing or harsh, have fragile confidence and resilience. They are lacking in initiative and tend to restrict themselves in their approaches to new situations. Today's parents can learn from the past. By blending the approaches of older generations with modern approaches, today's parents give their children the fundamental qualities required to be happy and successful adults. The modern parent's parenting philosophy must keep evolving because we know so much more than the older generations did. This new knowledge informs the way we parent our children today. We strive to be the best possible parents we can be.

It's impossible to prevent a child from experiencing the full range of human emotions or to protect them from every possible emotional upset. At times, kids are sad or anxious. They sometimes feel angry. They get tired, too. And, although we hate to admit it, children can also experience the less positive range of human emotions, including those feelings that make them uncomfortable, such as jealousy, hatred or even regret. Our goal as parents is not to prevent these feelings but to provide a safe, nurturing environment in which our kids can experience the full range of human emotions and learn how to handle them. The key point is to teach your child that it is okay to have these feelings, that every human does at some point or another. Our goal as parents is to let our children know that they are not alone; they always have someone they can confide in who will not judge or criticize, but will always love and console them.

3.1. Encouraging Self-expression

So how does one encourage self-expression without encouraging disrespect, in our often rule-bound, educative attempt to bring up socially conscious, moral individuals? It's tough; often the model answer isn't the only answer anymore; there isn't one. The truth is that no part of parenting is easy, and one's best attempt can be the best guide. Yet, it might help to remember that self-expression is not synonymous with disrespectful behavior, and that it can, in fact, be a rather positive quality in a person of any age. Just how can we encourage that habit of constructive self-expression? It's easier than you think. You will realize that when you next engage in a thoughtful debate on any subject. What we need to do sounds too simple to be true, but the problem is that most of us often forget to act as if we truly believe in the doctrine of equality. You truly need to believe that every human being has the same value as you do. This becomes especially tough when it comes to youngsters, given how much they're told what to do and think.

It's quite understandable that when children are small, we want to keep them safe by giving them strict rules of behavior and telling them what to do, and often what to think. At the same time, the strongest connection in our society is for individual freedom, liberty of behavior, thought, and expression. It may seem a tough balancing act to give your children space for self-expression, yet in today's rapidly globalizing and subtly shifting age, supple, creative, and open minds do seem to carry the day. They are precisely the ones who are usually seen enjoying themselves the most, who are more resourceful when it comes to challenges, and who contribute maximum, not least because their positive behavior rubs off on those around them.

3.2. Teaching Emotional Intelligence

While teaching our kids to write and read numbers, eat fruit, and stay active is important, teaching them to accept and respect oneself as well as get along with others is even more vital. One of the most important components of emotional intelligence is getting along with others. The modern fast-paced digital world often puts up barriers that make it much more difficult to naturally learn collaboration, compassion, and generosity. As always, teaching by example is the best first step. We ourselves have to be and to act just like the person we envision our child becoming. Guiding our kids with actively listening and showing enthusiasm for their interests, using a gentle, warm, and empathetic tone of voice, facilitating everyday collaborative opportunities, helping craft empathy-eliciting movies, and discussing others' situations, teaching culturally-governed body language and social roles from different cultures, and the emotional accents associated with them.

Some of the most important - yet sometimes neglected - lessons we can offer our children pertain to the importance of accepting and respecting oneself, as well as getting along with others (and, most importantly, recognizing other people's feelings). Among the most compelling findings on emotional self-awareness in children are that this trait predicts healthy social and emotional behaviors and that it is equally important for both boys and girls. Programs that help students to recognize and label their feelings have been seen to decrease negative behaviors and the prevalence of emotional symptoms in children. While there is currently little scientific evidence about the most effective way to nurture children's sense of confidence and self-worth, as parents we can surely find our unique recipe to foster our child's confidence by discussing feelings openly and empathetically using everyday situations to explain the impact of our children's actions on others, prioritize reading and discussing picture books that speak about emotions, make a point of appreciating our child's uniqueness, build our child's abilities through sharing decision making, offer positive thoughts, and empower our children... just to name a few possibilities. Remember - leading by example is another very effective approach!

3.3. Managing Stress and Anxiety

Sometimes children just need to talk about things that worry them. They can get a lot of comfort and reassurance from you. Many anxious children need direct lessons in how to handle anxiety when it gets to them. That are learning effective, long-term relaxation skills, even from an early age, will be better equipped to live an anxiety-free life. If your child is particularly nervous, you should start with deep breathing exercises. During a panic or anxiety attack, the breath pattern changes. These irregular, deep breaths can actually make the anxious feelings worse. To interrupt this cycle, teach your child to breathe slowly and deeply. Children may also benefit from learning that their body physically relaxes when they feel calm and safe. For mindfulness exercises, teach your child to close their eyes and simply focus on being aware of the rise and fall of their breath. This will help calm them as well.

How children deal with stress is a good predictor of whether they will suffer anxiety problems later on. If children react strongly to everyday challenges, they are more likely to develop anxiety disorders in the future. To protect our children from stress and anxiety, we want to be our happy, upbeat selves whenever we are with them. Then our warmth and optimism for life can be a comforting blanket that helps shield a child from the inevitable ups and downs of growing up. Fortunately, it doesn't mean we have to be perfect. For our children's sake, we don't need to hide all our woes, just make sure they don't know we are worrying about our worries.

CHAPTER 4

Fostering Confidence and Resilience

Humor, affection, respect, and dignity are four essential qualities the conscious parent uses every day. Wash your children with them and revel in the closeness it creates. Read Part 4 on warning signs and parent interventions when you notice that your child is vexed. Who would not want their children to be free from depression and anxiety, to have a quiet, resilient mind? Theoretical knowledge is important, too, but neither comes naturally. In order to have a strong, happy child, you need to understand them and to protect them from environmental vulnerabilities. Our research and the practices we recommend will help provide a structure in which your child will grow. But in the end, all your aspirations must live on your stick, love, and dignity.

Part 4 describes emotional difficulties and the risk factors and obstacles that can lead to their development. It gives you the symptoms of such basic emotional and personality problems as depression, anxiety disorder, bipolar disorder, personality disorder, substance use disorder, and more. The section demystifies these issues and offers symptoms of how a distressed child may show emotional and personality disorganization. It helps you to understand how a lack of appropriate self-protecting behavior may develop at home, at school, and amongst their friends, and what you can do to prevent the problem when your child is little and help them when they become a big person.

4.1. Setting Realistic Goals

As a parent, you can help your child plan a structured balance every day. Each part of the child's day can reflect the child and your family's individual beliefs and values. Maybe early morning is time for some mental focused time with various novels, easy things we will find something he/she will love to read to start the day with positive thoughts. FloatField's tests out your beliefs and values as they apply to the goals your family has in place. Help your child work up to their goals despite potential obstacles through adaptability, self-discipline, and resilience. Every child has the ability to develop these life skills or you can develop when living settings that enhance life skill development.

5 or 6 hours of challenging swim practice a week, however, can offer a source of support, camaraderie, and strength. Monte N, the son of a former employee, proved that "happiness" tops both gold medals and marathon practice. He became National Champ in Freestyle at Junior Nationals at 13 years old, took up the breaststroke at age 14 and became the fastest California breaststroker by age 17 with innovative swimming coach support. With joy and constancy he balanced academics, swimming, playing the guitar, and seeing the water of the world by age 16-18 signing language. Monte reminds us that overachievement can lead to grit and wonder, nature and nurture.

An ambitious overload of structured activities might be the preparation for a competitive world. Yet too much involvement in one or two sports or activities, the parent running "mileage" daily, can crowd out needed time for rest and informal free play, for exploration and wonder. When swimming practice also seems like a drudgereous, joyless burden, you might stop for a critical examination. Over-involvement in a single activity can cause the child to "self-deselect", and drop out for burnout or stress.

4.2. Encouraging Independence

Create new traditions that make small but significant changes in your family routine that help your child to want, respect and love each other. Tell them stories about where they come from and create family albums with the best memories. Deep down, teaching the child to love their family is the most important lesson in love and respect for ourselves and others. Always end the day on a positive note and celebrate your accomplishments, however small they are. Praise them and reward their effort. The idea is to build trust in the child's skills and help them want to continue advancing, learning and trying to improve.

The Uruguayan poet and essayist Juana de Ibarbourou once wrote that "loving children means letting them be children and not what we think they should be." Begin encouraging them to make their own choices. Let them choose the clothes they want to wear. Help them organize their room so that they know where all their clothes are instead of going through a "pre-chosen" outfit. Ask their opinion on small things and respect their ideas. Be patient and listen with genuine interest. It feels important to show the child that it is worth sharing with the family what they think or feel, in this way we are giving them confidence in their opinions and in themselves, we are not only validating what they express, but who they are, that is, that they count for themselves, not just for us.

4.3. Building a Growth Mindset

Children need to believe in themselves, learn strong coping skills for setbacks, and develop emotional resilience. They are most likely to accomplish these things when they have grown up in an environment that fosters self-esteem, one that does not set them up to feel defeated after a first blunder or bump in the road. In essence, kids who feel worthy, who have a growth mindset, seem to have been fortified with the personal attributes that can lessen the harshest emotional, social, and academic stress.

Parenting with Purpose: Nurturing happy, confident kids. The central message of Parenting with Purpose is that children need to believe that they are loved, wanted, and welcome, and that they are valued and valuable, as well as that they have the potential to achieve their dreams. Children who feel this way grow up to be happy, confident, and productive. When parents create an environment based on these principles, children learn they can ask for help without fear of disapproval or reprisal; they learn they can express concern without fear they will be called a tattler or a whiner; they learn that they can contribute to their group or community.

www.ingramcontent.com/pod-product-compliance
Lightning Source LLC
Chambersburg PA
CBHW020753150726
48196CB00023B/759